GED to MBA

By Andrea Norwood Walton

This book is dedicated to the village that helped me get here.

My mother, Urith Lynn Walker, grandmother, Gloria Walker,

and sister, Angelyn "Peaches" Norwood. My forever mentor,

Johnnie Payne. To my husband Gary and three heartbeats

Naiomi, Nachala and Gregory, I love you very much.

Chapter 1: Innocence Lost

Chapter 1: Innocence Lost

I have debated for years on whether to fully share my story. Some parts are painful to relive and it makes me extremely vulnerable, however, I pray it inspires you regardless of your upbringing, your socioeconomic status or the color of your skin to push beyond your comfort and be great. You can overcome and succeed. Will this be easy? Hell No! Will it be worth it? Absolutely! As I reflect on where I am today, I know statistically I am not supposed to be here but thank God I am.

I do not despise my journey, on the contrary, I am who I am today because of my journey and the village that has supported and prayed for me along the way. Winning in life is not the absence of the tough times it is despite them. Know when you also face tough times, it is by those you are defined. I was born and raised in Southern California, specifically, Pasadena. My mom tells me the day I was born she and my dad were grocery shopping because she was so hungry. Once they got back to the apartment, he gave her a piggy-back ride up the stairs because she could not make it. Once upstairs, her water broke. She says she was somewhat upset because she was very hungry and just bought a lot of food. Not long after I was born, my mom and dad divorced. I know in hindsight this was not an easy decision for my mom but her peace of mind and joy was more important for her and for us.

We moved to a back house on Lincoln Ave in Pasadena; we had a yard, a garden and a dog. It was a small house but it was home. At four years old, a close family member lured both my sister and I and forced us both to engage in a sex act. I remember feeling scared and confused. I also remember feeling like I could not say a word, not even to my mother. It happened again not long after, it was the beginning of this constant need for validation, and the feeling of "not enough," this would be my cross to bear. Being sexualized at such a young age caused me over the years to equate my value with sex and not the totality of who I am. Eventually, we shared with our mom what happened but it took years of feeling resentful and depressed to share. I am still working through these feelings and if I had to guess, it may take a lifetime but I am working through them.

As a child, I would pray and beg God to take the hard times away. I could not understand that an all-powerful, all-knowing God would allow suffering and struggle. I have since matured spiritually but it was a tough concept as a little girl. I did not want us to worry about having enough money, having enough food, my mom working late hours and multiple jobs. One of my mom's jobs was a radio disc jockey for years on a gospel show. Out of the jobs she had, she really loved this one. Sometimes if she worked graveyard, she would take my sister and I with her. It felt like an adventure, we would have blankets on the floor of the radio station while my mom did her show. Now as I am older, I understand some choices she made to keep moving us forward. It is funny; I remember the Publisher's Clearing House Sweepstakes commercials with Ed McMahon. Peaches and I would ask our mom to play the sweepstakes so we would win millions and move out of the neighborhood. We would watch the night they would reveal who won with hopes they would knock on our door. Of course, they did not but we loved to envision better for our family. I did not want the struggle because it brought uncertainty and at that age, fear.

My immediate family is small, my grandmother, Gloria Walker (deceased), mom, Urith Walker, my sister (Peaches) and brother (Phillip). My mother worked hard, she was always resilient and a firm believer in God, prayer, and family. I also saw the fatigue in her eyes. We went to church every Sunday, bible study mid-week and choir rehearsals. In the early 80s, we moved to Community Arms Apartments. We loved the new place; it was a big departure from the back house we lived in on Lincoln. At that age, we never knew what we were missing; my mom was good that way. My sister Peaches and I played outside and formed lifelong friendships. We had what we needed and there was one commonality in our neighborhood with most of us kids, absent fathers, and so it made our bonds stronger. We would commiserate about how they were not there or when they did say they would come pick us up, it was a big deal. Often the latter never happened but it felt good to talk about the possibilities.

Our community had its issues but it was like most low-income communities back in the 80s. We also had our share of scary times; we would play tag with the police sirens in the background. I remember literally following the blood drops of someone stabbed the night before while playing outside. There was one day all the kids were playing and a shoot-out happened between rival gangs. I hid next to the slides and once the shooting subsided, I ran home. No matter how often this happened, once it died down, we would be right back outside playing. It was a mix of hopefulness and sadness but it was ours. Free summer lunches, the sounds of the fellas on the basketball court, birds chirping and a community that looked out for each other. Some of my favorite and most memorable childhood memories came from Community Arms.

My father was not in our lives, he was emotionally and physically absent. For years, he lived around the corner from us and still was not there. I still struggle with this because the love I have for my children, I cannot imagine not being there for them but this was my reality.

Lesson 1: Sometimes you will experience circumstances that change who you are. Find the Light even in the darkness.

Chapter 2: Daddy Issues

Chapter 2: Daddy issues

The bond between a father and his daughter is one I will never know or understand. I am blessed that throughout my life I have had a village of Godly men, namely my Uncle Daryl, who have spoken into my life. Over the years, the connection with my own father is what I have longed for. There was one day my dad had arranged with my mom that he would pick my sister and I up to spend time, we were so excited. He told my mom he would be there around noon. I did not want to take a chance on missing him so I sat on the back stairs of our apartment that faced Orange Grove Blvd and waited.

It was a beautiful Southern California day; the sun was out and I watched cars pass repeatedly. Any car that looked like my dad's, I would perk up. After a couple of hours, nothing. My mom peeked out the door and asked if I wanted to come back in. I was determined and said,

"No, my dad is on his way." Another couple of hours passed and I was still sitting. My mom peeked out again, I got this feeling in the pit of my stomach but I stayed there sitting on the stairs. By around 6 pm it was dark and my mom said, "Andrea come on back in." It was just a few stairs but the longest walk back ever. How could he not show up? Does he not love me? What did I do? I cried as I went back in. This round of rejection stung and became an open wound for me for years to come.

My preteen years were a pivotal time for me. This age for anyone is fragile and when you add abuse and rejection, I questioned my worth. My father lived around the corner from us in a tiny yellow house on Painter Street. Every day, I took the city bus, the RTD (Regional Transportation District) to and from school. The path I would take would lead me right past my father's home. Often as I walked by, he would be home, door open and screen closed sitting on his couch. He would watch me walk by and sometimes he waved other times no acknowledgment. Every day I walked by I hoped for a different response from him. I guess I could have gone around a different way but I wanted him to want me. I saw how other dads responded to their daughters, I didn't have that.

For a few years during that period, he was trying to reconcile with my mom. I always felt he wanted my mom over our family. However, the possibility we could one day be a family again is all my sister and I ever wanted. He moved in with us at some point and I could not believe that he would be there when I got home from school every day. I shared with our friends that our dad had come home with excitement this was a big deal. The reconciliation, however, was short-lived. I came home and found a handwritten letter "To Lynn and the girls," I read the letter and cried. He said he had to leave, he said he had another life. He could not live up to what my mom demanded of him and moving in with us was a mistake. I became used to him saying one thing and doing another.

Some months later, he said he had moved into a townhome close by and I could come and visit. I always tracked him down. It is funny no matter how often he let me down; I would risk disappointment yet again. I told my mom and although it was getting dark, I wanted to go see him. I walked to his place and knocked on the door, someone else answered. I thought maybe I got it wrong house so I knocked on all of the doors in the complex, he was not there. I kept knocking in hopes to see his face and to see happiness in his eyes. Another sting. He did not actually live there but that is what he told me.

In junior high, I got my first job at the Rose Bowl Aquatics Center as a locker room attendant. I have always had a great work ethic, showing up early every day. I would sweep and mop floors, clean toilets and pick up after the more affluent in Pasadena. I always envisioned myself successful even though I did not know how exactly to get there. I went to John Marshall Fundamental and sometimes I walked home from school, a good forty-five-minute walk but I liked walking through the nice neighborhoods. Often if there was a large home for sale and I saw the "Open House" sign, I would make a detour and take a tour by myself. It was always so funny to see the agent's face, I'd walk in and they would look around and say, "Are you here alone?" and every time I would say yes, I'd like a tour and sure enough they would oblige. I would envision myself in these homes. Where my room would be, where my mom and sister's rooms would be. I even kept a list of the goals I wanted to achieve on school paper and committed to myself as I accomplished, I would check them off. I always saw myself accomplishing great things both personally and professionally, I just had to figure out how to get there.

I was horribly bullied in junior high. My grades suffered and I had a hard time focusing. Sometimes, I was spit on, locker broken into several times and once my teacher asked me to go to another class and pass on a message. I opened the door and all of the eyes turned toward me. As I inched my way to the teacher, the class laughed at my shoes and hair. I never really felt like I fit in. I was tall, lanky and sort of a nerd. One day I was on the bus heading home and the "cool kids" sat in the back. One did not dare go to the back unless you had the right shoes and outfit on and in the hierarchy of cool, I knew I was way at the bottom. The only seat available was near the back door of the bus. I heard the kids laughing and talking about my hair, clothes, and shoes. I had gotten used to the snickers. I pulled the string to let the driver know I needed to get off the bus and before the bus came to a full stop, someone threw a small plastic cup of salsa on me. It literally went from my hair and down my clothes. The bus seemed to erupt in laughter; I got off and walked home crying.

I was depressed and had suicidal thoughts. I routinely drew pictures of me dying, I collected the pills my mom had with a glass of water and contemplated dying. The pain of rejection caused me to think I was not worth living. I wanted something or someone to ease the pain. As I grew taller (5'8 at fourteen) and blossomed, so did the attention I got from boys and men. At fourteen, I met a senior at my high school who played football and gave me the attention I desperately needed.

Lesson: Sometimes the thing you need is not supposed to come from the person you think.

Chapter 3: Mom at Fifteen

Chapter 3: Mom at Fifteen

I dated this high school football player and I instantly fell in love. Now looking back, I know I was just a conquest for him but for me, it was literally everything. I spent a lot of time after school and on the weekends with him. He was my first and I finally felt wanted and needed however soon things changed quickly. My period was over a month late and I knew I was pregnant. I was in denial and went on for about four months without telling anyone. I snuck my Medi-Cal stickers from my mom and finally decided to walk to our pediatrician's office on my own to check. I asked for a pregnancy test and my doctor walked in and said disappointedly, "If you are, what are you going to do?" I could not speak; I was so scared and discouraged. I did not know what I was going to do. The test came back positive and I walked home crying. From then on, it was baggie clothes and sitting with pillows hiding my stomach. I finally got the courage and told my mother over the next couple of weeks.

I said, "Mom, I have to tell you something," and she looked at me and said with disappointment and sadness in her eyes, "You're pregnant." I nodded my head yes slowly. She held my hand with tears and said, "Why, Andrea?" I had let her down. My life I thought was over. I thought I was ready to be married and have my family. My daughter's father was moving away to Ohio and I pleaded with my mother to let me move with him and his family. Even his mom called my mom and asked. My mother stood her ground and said absolutely not. I yelled at my mom, I cried and I was angry. I cannot thank my mom enough for sticking to her guns and saying no. One of the best decisions made for me.

We discovered I had a high-risk pregnancy so I stopped going to school. We moved right before I gave birth in Montclair, CA. A fresh start with my mom, sister, and grandmother. The day I went into labor was surreal. We had to drive back to Pasadena so I could deliver at Huntington Hospital. I did not know how to feel but I knew this was my reality. I was in labor for thirty-six hours and my daughter was born at 8:16 am March 3, 1992, with my mom and sister by my side. She was also born with a disability, a radial club hand. I had no idea the entire time I was pregnant that she would be different. When they brought her to me swaddled, the doctor came in and unwrapped her and said simply, "She was born with a radial club hand, go to Children's Hospital when she turns one." He wrapped her back up, handed her to me and walked out. Not only was I a mom but I did not know how to handle this news and what was a radial club hand anyway? I knew I loved her so much. The distance between where I was and where I wanted my life was so vast I did not know if I would ever be what I saw in my mind. Just because things look different from the vision that God gave you, does not mean it will not come to pass.

I applied for welfare benefits so I could go to school and support my daughter. As I stood in line for food stamps and medical coverage, I remember I had dressed up. I had on full makeup and a nice outfit as though I was going to a job interview vs. needing help. I remember looking down at my clothes and thinking I was overdressed but I wanted to let them know in my own way, I would not need this long.

Once she turned one year, I reached out to Los Angeles Children's Hospital. I was sixteen and overwhelmed. I remember my caseworker, Jamie Black; she was amazing by the way and walked me through Naiomi's disability. Essentially, Naiomi was born without a thumb on her right hand and an arm that was folded inward. She would endure a lot of pain and surgeries in her little life. I blamed myself as a young mom for having a daughter born different. I would do a lot of self-talk like, "I should have gone to the doctor sooner," "I wasn't taking vitamins early on," "I am a horrible mother." I battled with Medi-Cal constantly to make sure she had medical coverage for her surgeries. There were nights at the hospital or at home when I held her and wept. This mountain of anxiety, fear, and low self-esteem felt insurmountable. As I reflect on that time, I went from being a child to a mom in fifteen years. I never experienced the typical teen years, which is why I often feel older than I am. I sped past that quickly into adulthood.

Lesson 3: You do not have to look like where you are, dust yourself off and keep going.

Chapter 4: Reality vs. Aspirations

Chapter 4: Reality vs. Aspirations

We moved to Upland, CA a year later and I got a job as a waiter at Bullwinkle's Pizza, miniature golf and arcade games. I also dropped out of high school to help take care of my daughter and take more hours on at my job. I had learned how to deal with my new reality. My daughter would have ten surgeries over her life to correct her hand and scoliosis. My mom and sister were right there. There were a lot of long hospital nights and seeing Naiomi in pain. She wore many casts as a toddler and splints. She was and is resilient and I admire her so much. I just wanted her to be ok, I did not want people to stare and ask questions. I knew she would have to deal with people that are not so kind in her life. We learned together. After getting settled in as a new mom, her father resurfaced in our lives when she was six months old and promised he would help me and make it work. I still believed I could have a family, especially for my daughter. I became pregnant again at sixteen. I hated myself for not doing better and allowing myself to be in this place. I was already on welfare, how was I going to support two children? I struggled with the decision to keep my child; ultimately, I did not and had an abortion at sixteen. Shortly thereafter, we broke up and he moved away to Oakland. I have not seen him in years and Naiomi, unfortunately, has no relationship with her father. This ugly cycle continued with me, a cycle I promised would be different with me.

I knew I had to get my high school diploma to have a better life for Naiomi. Working as a waitress would not take care of us and my hours were being cut. I started going to a continuation High School and working. It was difficult to balance work, school and my daughter but I did for a while. I made some friends and was feeling like a normal high schooler. I was a year behind but I was going and that is what mattered. There was a guy who I had a crush on who approached me and told me he was having a house party and was inviting some friends over. I wanted to go and my mom had to work, so my grandmother agreed to watch Naiomi for me. My mom said she would drop me off on her way to work at the radio station overnight. I got dressed, crop top, short shorts, and combat boots, totally 90s gear. We pulled up and the house seemed quiet but I assumed I was early. My mom asked if I was ok and I assured her I was, I knew I could get a ride home from friends.

I walked up to the door and knocked. The guy who invited me was there. There was no music, no food, and no people. The TV was on and I sat on the couch. I asked what was going on and where everyone was. He kept telling me other friends were on their way. After about twenty minutes, he sat next to me, he begin touching me, and tried to kiss me. I was angry and kept trying to push him off; he grabbed my shorts and tried to take them off. I yelled, "Stop! I am leaving." I grabbed my purse and left. The problem was, I had no ride home because we had one car and I had no money. So at almost midnight, I walked home, in short shorts and a crop top. I was roughly seven or eight miles away from home, so in what felt like forever, I walked all night. I had men slowly driving by me the entire night. I kept praying and crying. I was cold and afraid. I remember passing by a gas station and a car slowly drove out and followed me for a couple of blocks. Thankfully, I always walked in the opposite direction of traffic so I could see what was coming. There were streets with no sidewalk or no lights. Once I finally got to my street at Benson and Foothill in Upland, CA, I was close and I ran the rest of the way. I thank God to this day I made it home safe. I stopped going to that Continuation school. I could not keep up and I did not want to see this guy anymore. I then registered to take the GED test at nineteen. I studied for weeks and registered for the test. I was so nervous because a few months prior I had taken the California High School Proficiency Exam and failed. I knew this had to happen, I was running out of options. We had no car but I had a twelve-speed bike and during both days, it rained so hard. I rode my bike several miles to take the test and the next day rode my bike again. I got home drenched, hoping and praying I would pass. Several weeks later, I received notification in the mail I passed! You cannot imagine the joy and relief I felt. Oh my goodness, finally there was light at the end of the tunnel, a chance to start to carve out the life I wanted.

Now at nineteen years old, I had my GED, I got a job as a retail rep at a Rent-A-Center and I was making $16 an hour. Back then that was a lot of money and I just bought my first car, a Dodge Monaco. Things were looking up and I felt like I was finally on track. On my third day on my new job, a couple of guys came in during the afternoon to look at jewelry (yes they rented jewelry) and I walked up and asked if they needed help. They both shrugged me off and said nothing, I thought nothing of it and assisted other customers.

Later during my closing shift with my supervisor, we were helping our final few customers; one customer had two little girls with him, both were under ten years old. Behind the counter was a desk and I was sitting there making some final calls to customers about their bill. I heard the front door of the store abruptly open and three armed and masked gunmen ran in yelling for us to get down. Initially, I was paralyzed, everything slowed way down and I could not move. One of them put the gun in my face and told me to get down, I did. I heard the little girls screaming and crying. Their father was desperately trying to console them. I thought for sure we would all die. I just remember being on the ground in a fetal position with the paperwork I was completing covering my face, shaking. All I could see was the barrel of the shotgun and his boots standing over me. I just wanted them to leave. In what seemed like forever, a few moments later they left. I laid on the floor crying and when we finally got up, the store manager called the police. They came and took statements from the employees and customers. I always thought in hindsight the men that came in earlier were casing the store. They had no interest in speaking with me and walked around the store a couple of times. During a team meeting a few days later, I asked my supervisor Cassandra what steps would be taken to mitigate robberies in the future. She told me, "This is a risk you take working in retail." I quit the same day; that is a risk I was not willing to take. During that same year, my sister was stabbed with a box cutter at school multiple times by a girl who was jealous of her who she thought was her best friend. To walk into the hospital room and see my sister bandaged up, I can only describe as unreal and heartbreaking. Thank God she survived and her strength, resilience and crazy sense of humor is amazing. One day she will tell her story and it will blow folks' minds. That was a very tough year for my mom and for our entire family.

I took on another job as an assistant at an insurance agency and another job at the West Covina Mall at a women's retail chain while going to school part-time. During my time at the insurance agency, I sometimes had no babysitter for my daughter so I would bring her to work at the Insurance Company. I would have a blanket and toys and she would sit at my desk on the floor. There were times I did not have money for food so I would take someone else's lunch out of the break room. Horrible, I know but I was desperate.

During this time, I also aspired to model. The early 90s when Naomi Campbell and Cindy Crawford dominated the runways and magazine covers, I just knew I could do that too. I would practice my runway walk in my bedroom and daydream about someday being on the real runway. The reality of my situation and my aspirations were always at odds. I had done local beauty pageants; the first one was Young American Stars. I came in second place and wanted to go to the next level. Although I lived in Pasadena, I was eligible to go after Miss West Covina, which could then possibly lead to Miss California. I was excited and was preparing feverishly for the pageant. I bought a beautiful, brown sparkly dress that matched my brown skin. I knew that was the dress when I saw it in the store window. I bought satin shoes from Payless and had them dyed to match the dress.

Just a few weeks before the pageant, officials asked us to write a summary of our lives for the pageant booklet, essentially an introduction. I completed the summary and included that I was a teen mom, working hard and going to school. I promptly received a call that I could not participate because I had a daughter as a teen and it did not align with the message and values they wanted to send to young women. I was devastated because I felt this would be my ticket to a better life, another opportunity gone, but I am a born fighter so I kept going. I had been sending photos to agents in L.A. and New York with little success. My mom would drive me around and take me on "Go-Sees" and I was consistently told, "We have someone already that looks like you," "You're too dark," "You need to move to New York, you can't do commercial." I finally signed with an agent in Beverly Hills but looking back I was so desperate to be signed; I agreed to an exclusive contract (never, ever do exclusive) and I had very few jobs to show for it.

I finally spent money on some incredible photos with this amazing local photographer, Tracy Caan. She helped transform even how I felt about myself and the photos were amazing. The day of the photo shoot I was nervous, I knew this investment had to pay off. I took a chance and mailed them to Ebony Magazine in Chicago. I had not heard anything in weeks, so I figured I was not what they wanted.

I was at work at the insurance agency when I received a phone call and a message from Ebony Magazine. They had a historic traveling runway show, Ebony Fashion Fair, and they wanted me to come out for auditions for the 40th-anniversary tour. What?! As you can imagine my mind was blown. I went home and told my mom immediately and she was so happy for me, finally, something panned out. At the same time, we had to move back with my grandmother because finances for my mom were getting tough. Soon after, I received my airline ticket from Ebony with my itinerary. I just sat and stared at the ticket with Shirley Horn's "Here's to Life" playing in the background, I could not believe it. A few weeks later, I flew to Chicago and the experience alone was enough but when I got to the building on Michigan Ave and saw the covers of this amazing magazine in my home for years I was speechless. This magazine was the epitome and epicenter of black culture and style for decades.

We got upstairs; there was a room of about fifty or so young women and men. They called us in groups. As you can imagine, the room was packed with young and absolutely stunning black men and women. They finally called my name to go walk in front of the panel that included Eunice Johnson, the founder of Ebony Fashion Fair and the wife of the publisher John H. Johnson. I walked for my life! I needed this break, my family needed this break, and this had to happen. We all waited in a room and they finally came out began calling names. My name was one of the last names called and the room applauded for those selected. We were immediately whisked away downstairs and took our first photos for Jet Magazine; this was Top Model before Top Model was a show. I called my mom immediately and told her, she was so happy for me and she agreed to keep Naiomi for me for nine months while I traveled and modeled. I sent my money home to my mom regularly to help support Naiomi and the household. I arrived in Chicago in mid-August of 1997 with my one suitcase and maybe three pairs of shoes. I was still amazed that this would be my life. We checked into the Essex hotel, next door to Johnson's Publishing Company. For several weeks we practiced, we had fittings and we bonded. To this day, I am still good friends with many of the models. I would call my mom, grammie, and Naiomi from the road a lot, I missed them so much. One day I called home and my grammie just cried. I ask if she was ok and I told her I loved her, she said I love you too. It was time to pack up from the Essex and take the shows on the road.

The shows were in front of thousands and this is where I learned how to hold court, to walk like I owned the room and to be courageous. The clothes were gorgeous, Dolce & Gabbana, L'Amour and B. Michael just to name a few.

One day while traveling through Mobile, Alabama I received a call from my mom that my grammie had passed away in her sleep. It was one of the worst days of my life. I went home for her funeral and spent time with my family. Grammie was the glue, the matriarch of our family. She was a fighter, she was a lady and she played no games. Thinking about her makes me smile.

My mom loved her and she was in so much pain when grammie passed away. I learned a few days before her death she was cleaning the house and singing "He's Preparing Me" by Daryl Coley. She knew and I believe she was ready. I left and finished the tour with Ebony, 180 cities domestically and internationally. I traveled places I only dreamed of and for this, I will forever be grateful.

Once the tour was over I wanted to keep going, I auditioned for TV shows, did some small gigs in L.A. but it could never get off the ground like I wanted. I created a video for an audition BET (Black Entertainment Television) was having for a show called "Teen Summit." The show was for African American youth and tackled the societal issues we faced as a community. I mailed the video and received a letter that they wanted me to come in person. I was thrilled the only problem was I needed $500 for an airline ticket to get to D.C. We did not have it and another opportunity gone. The following year we lost the house we were living in. My mom was renting and the homeowners sold it right from under us. We had thirty days to find a place to live. I pulled out my phone book and called around. I called an older woman at our church who let us live with her for $300 a month. After three months, I found an apartment and started working for Macy's at the Estee Lauder cosmetics counter. I hustled and hustled hard to take care of my little girl.

Lesson 4: Do what is necessary to keep moving forward. Winning requires persistence, even when you are tired.

Chapter 5: Wins and Losses

Chapter 5: Wins and Losses

Because I wanted validation, I dated men that were all over the spectrum, those that seemed to have it together, those that wished they had it together and those that could never get it together. I wanted the ideal marriage and relationship and this always seemed to elude me. Do not get it twisted, I am far from perfect, however, the problem was I was not sure what that looked like for me. I needed my father to model the right behaviors early on and because he did not, dating was like playing "pin the tail on the donkey." I had blind spots and always seemed to miss the mark. I met and married my second daughter's father after only knowing him for three months. I worked as a bank teller at local credit union and we got pregnant and had Nachala almost immediately. It felt like I finally had what I always wanted. On July 14, 2000, I was in labor for twelve hours with her and in a different place in my life. Her little face was perfect and she gave me a second chance at motherhood. If Naiomi was my daughter where I was trying to figure motherhood out, Nachala was the daughter when I felt more prepared to be a mom. She was and is her father's twin. Headstrong and a "take no prisoners" attitude, she was born determined. She marches to the beat of her own drum and dares you to question her steps. Now married, I wanted to create that family for both girls. I joke that Naiomi is my daughter that is sweet and for the most part agreeable. Nachala equally as sweet, but boy oh boy, a firecracker since birth, she keeps me on my toes. I was a different mom after her birth to both girls. The things I did not get a chance to do with Naiomi because I was so young or could not afford it; I was able to do with both girls. After almost four years of what was clearly not a good fit for us, we divorced. We have a beautiful daughter from that union and if that was the sole purpose, I am grateful. After the divorce, I had started working for a temp agency making $12 hour and taking care of two girls, rent, and utilities on that wage.

I did not have a college degree so I went back to the credit union and I was a call center representative. It was the first job where I learned how to operate in a corporate setting and learn to be politically agile; it was one of my favorite jobs. When you can demonstrate leadership, do so. You do not have to have manager or leader in your title. I demonstrated leadership even in the call center and was promoted three times in one year and finally ended up as the administrative assistant to the CEO.

I decided I would go back to school to get my degree. Getting my undergrad seemed almost out of reach but I always saw myself completing it, so I decided I would go. There were long days and nights, sleep deprivation and some stress because there was no going back for me. I chose the University of Phoenix because the campus was close to my job and the program was perfect for me while juggling both my girls and work. My decision to work during the day and go to school at night proved to be a huge sacrifice for my girls and I. Naiomi would watch Nachala on school nights and I would study on the weekends. There were times when I did not think I could finish, times where it did not feel like it would pay off. The money I was making was just enough to pay the rent and there were a couple of times I could not pay the light bill or pulled together just enough for food. I am grateful for my landlords at the time they were so gracious and knew how hard I was working. I was late almost every month with the rent but it got paid. This was my motivation to finish and I promised myself I would never be at the mercy of anyone ever again. I knew ultimately, I would have a career I loved and through God's grace created success for me and my girls.

In 2006, I graduated with a Bachelor's of Science in Criminal Justice; I wanted to practice law at some point. My daughters, my mom, and sister in the stands cheering me on. I could not have done it without them. The counselor at school asked me, "Why stop? Get your MBA." Now that getting my undergrad was complete, getting my MBA would be icing and it would take me just two years. I was already in work/school mode so, I kept going and two years later received my degree. To say the journey was hard is an understatement but I did it. I pushed myself to the point sometimes where it was uncomfortable. My friends kept me accountable and when I looked at my girls, that was all the motivation I needed. I then started in Human Resources as a recruiter at the Credit Union. I had no experience but the VP of HR, Michelle Esser took a chance on me and I will forever be grateful to her. I was sitting outside of the CEO's office and she walked up to me and said, "I have a recruiter role I think you would be great at." I had never even considered it but I loved Human Resources and it seemed to be a great fit for who I am. A few years later, Coca-Cola called and I accepted a role with them as a Recruiter. It was the first time I had a job where I traveled and I was based out of Los Angeles. I was finally making enough money to take my daughters on small trips and splurge on us. Learning how to operate in corporate America was a different experience for me. However, I had taken some of those life lessons of survival and resiliency and applied that to the day-to-day. If a colleague would say, "That's a tough manager, good luck", "can you build out a strategy?" or "Are you sure you can take on that group?" In my mind, I am thinking, if you knew what I had to fight to get here, you would understand why getting this done does not seem to be much of an obstacle for me.

Lesson 5: Forgiveness releases you and when you are healing and whole that is all that matters.

Chapter 6: Personal Triumph

Chapter 6: Personal Triumph

I desired to address some of the root causes of my feelings; I began to see a therapist to deal with the demons I had kept under wraps for so long. I was still very hurt but until I dealt with the pain, I could not develop healthy relationships. I went for a couple of years, forgave, and began to heal. I still believe in therapy tune-ups, this is definitely not a one and done type of healing.

Now that I had my MBA, I felt fearless that I could apply for any role and I would be hired. I also felt more in control, no more were things just happening to me and that goes back to what I experienced growing up. Some unfortunate things *happened* to me; I was now in a position where I was creating an opportunity for myself. I was learning the corporate ropes, how to build relationships and become politically agile. I had now been in Human Resources for a few years and I wanted to take on meatier roles. I needed to help lead a business and people to take my career to the next level. I had to "cut my teeth" and I did that at Target. I was the HR manager of a store in the Valley (outside of Los Angeles) for almost two years and I learned quickly being a leader does not happen behind your desk. I pushed pallets of product with employees while catching up with them on how they were doing personally and professionally. I would also work graveyard shift with the logistics team, engaging the employees and being present. Where I grew up, I learned along the way that you chip in whenever possible and that is how I have tried to lead along the way. This role was the one I needed to catapult me to the next level. From Target, I was then recruited over to Nestle USA as an HR business partner. This role came at the perfect time, it was much closer to home, I was there more for my girls and I had my weekends back. I will be at Nestle USA for seven years in 2018. I have learned over my career you must establish credibility early for your teams and leadership to buy in. Folks ask me all the time, "What does it take to be successful?" There is no secret sauce, it is:

1. Have a plan. We have all heard the phrase "if you fail to plan, you plan to fail."

2. Do what you said you would do. Nothing is worse than going back on your word.

3. Take accountability. OWN your stuff (I would use another word but you get it).

4. Build relationships. You are not an island and you NEED others to survive.

5. Give back. What have you learned that can help someone else?

6. Always be a student and continue learning. Whether that is a seminar, class or a mentor.

In 2016, I started my own nonprofit, Walton HR Consulting – HR for the Community. I hosted career sessions for job seekers throughout Southern California. I believed what I had learned over the years was valuable and insider info for job seekers. As I hosted these sessions, I learned there was a real hunger out there for people to prepare themselves for interviews and ultimately the careers they wanted. In addition, I have spoken with non-profits that support young women and teen moms to share my story hoping to help them see they can and will do great things in their own lives. I am now finishing up a job seeker app that can take what I teach in those sessions to bite-sized info on the go.

Nestle relocated to Virginia in 2017 and I was offered the opportunity to relocate with my family and bought a home for the first time, which has been a blessing. It looks just like the homes I would stop in on my way home from school when I was twelve. I envisioned it, spoke it and never let it go. A die-hard Southern California girl, now on the East Coast. Who would have thought?

I am now remarried to Gary Walton for almost seven years, we have a four-year-old son Gregory, my girls have grown up beautifully (Naiomi is an author in her own right and Nachala has been accepted to three universities as I write this book). In addition, my career in Human Resources is blossoming, over fifteen years in the field and I am excited about what God is doing in my life. Oh, and that list I created years ago with my goals, I still have it. It is tattered and worn now but happy to say, almost everything is checked off my list. I have now upgraded my list to the IPad and added new goals for this next chapter of my life – so stay tuned!

I want to further build upon the legacy of my grandmother and mother of women who never give up as well as providing a different life than the one I had for my children. So my children can go after their dreams and goals without some of the obstacles I faced. It has been a remarkable journey and I am just getting started. This little brown girl from Pasadena is a warrior, a survivor, and charting my own path to success and so can you!

To that young person who doubts himself or herself, to the divorcee who is not sure they can start again, to that single mom that cries alone. I see you, I was you and you will make it to the other side. Do not give up!

Lesson: Keep living and keep striving for greatness.

Made in the USA
Monee, IL
17 May 2020